reasons To be happy at The beach

reasons to be happy
at the beach

by Sandy Gingras

DOWN THE SHORE
PUBLISHING
Harvey Cedars, New Jersey

Down The Shore Publishing Corp.
Box 3100, Harvey Cedars, NJ 08008

www.down-the-shore.com

The words "Down The Shore" and the Down The Shore Publishing logo
are a registered U.S. Trademark.

Printed in China
4 6 8 10 9 7 5 3

Library of Congress Cataloging-in-Publication Data

Gingras, Sandy, 1958-
Reasons to be happy at the beach / by Sandy Gingras.
p. cm.
ISBN 0-945582-98-6
1. Gingras, Sandy, 1958---Catalogs. 2. Beaches in art--Catalogs. I. Title.

ND1839.G52 2003
700'.92--dc21

2003046191

We are raised on the idea of the pursuit of happiness. But pursuit is such a hard word. It suggests that happiness is something for our future, that we have to climb toward or race for, or earn in some struggly way. But, as I wrote

This book, I realized how present happiness really is. How it's all around us. We're looking right at it, breathing it in, holding it in our hands. It's in a gesture or a slant of light. It's a little piece of now.

And it's already ours.. There are so many reasons to be happy at the beach. All we have to do is notice ...

the first step
over the dune

holding a baby
in The waves

the sound that
flip-flops make

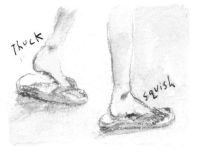

Thuck

squish

white

corn

the gray
rumbly Line

of a sTorm coming

that salty smell

the winding creek
Through The marsh

a sky full of geese

surfers

in flowered shorTs

dribble castles

going out To The sandbar

when you find a white feather

dolphins coming in close

the way crabs
walk sideways

the crush of
waves in The
nigh T

whaT is weathered

geTTing The besT carousel horse

a fisherman's back

a bobber bobbing

rain thaT sheeTs sideways

Tan Lines

an outSide shower

a sliver of
sunseT LeFT

what washes up

sand even in your pockets

when The eLasTic
sTarTs To go

the big LobSTer poT

The clank of a
sailboat line
on a stormy day

how explorers
must have feLT

shells on the window sill

the miniature golf hole
where The ball goes Through
the clown mouth, around
The maze, down The Tunnel
and inTo The hole

sTaying in so Long
ThaT your fingers Turn
inTo   prunes

The way
dune grass leans

a far casT

toads hopping under
a sTreeTLighT

a blowfish belly
all puffed up

paper plaTes

Sun bleached
bones

really red watermelon

finding clams with your feet

the murky achey smell
of low tide

catching one

when The TurTles hatch

the sound of
a LiTTLe engine
heading ouT

how STiLL an
egreT STands

crushes

when the moon
makes a silver path

moths around
The porch LighT

funny shaped Toes

when the lifeguards leave

LeTTing a KiTe
go up faST

a silvery school
of minnows

S no-cones

The Sound of The Shell windchimes

waTching Them
cLean The fish

crooked pilings

how fast the
fog comes in

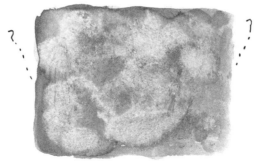

one wave afTer anoTher

when The Tide
goes way ouT

pulling up The crab Trap

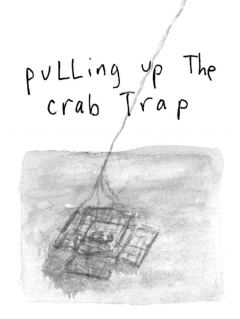

how the air smells
when you water
the TomaToes

blue beach glass

finding
crickeTs under
a board

when The bail
cLicks over

a good book
on a rainy day

peaches in a bowl

the front porch swing

the crooked way you feel
trying To walk in Someone
else's footprints

your secret fishing spot

how seagulls
hunch up in the wind

going through
The rusty gate

when you
leT Things go

The way sound carries

starry starry nights

The wind
at your back

reeLing in

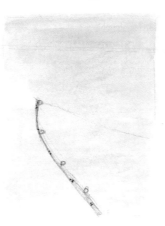

reasons of your own...

About the Author

Sandy Gingras is an artist and writer with her own design company called "How To Live" (visit her website at www.how-to-live.com). She and her son and two cats live near the beach on an island in New Jersey, where she is active in efforts to preserve open space and wetlands.

If you liked this book, you'll also enjoy these other books by Sandy Gingras:

How to Live on an Island   ISBN 0-945582-57-9

How to Live at the Beach   ISBN 0-945582-73-0

In a House by the Sea   ISBN 1-59322-013-8

The Uh-oh Heart   ISBN 0-945582-96-X

How to be a Friend   ISBN 0-945582-99-4

At the Beach House - A Guest Book   ISBN 1-59322-006-5

The annual How to Live at the Beach: Year Round Calendar

Down The Shore Publishing offers other book and calendar titles (with a special emphasis on the coast). For a free catalog, or to be added to our mailing list, just send us a request.

Down The Shore Publishing
P.O. Box 3100 ❖ Harvey Cedars, NJ 08008
or email: info@down-the-shore.com
www.down-the-shore.com